ATTR

A CHANGE OF AFFECTION

All It Takes Is That One Thing

Shannon Glover

Table of Contents

Chapter 1: 6 Tips To Find The One 6

Chapter 2: 9 New Date Ideas That Will Deepen Your Relationship 10

Chapter 3: 7 Ways To Live Together In Harmony With Your Partner 13

Chapter 4: 7 Signs You're More Attractive Than You Think 17

Chapter 5: 6 Ways To Attract Anything You Want In Life 22

Chapter 6: 6 Habits of Strong Couples 26

Chapter 7: 8 Ways To Love Yourself First 30

Chapter 8: 8 Signs Someone Misses You 34

Chapter 9: 6 Signs You Have A Fear of Intimacy 37

Chapter 10: 6 Ways To Flirt With Someone 41

Chapter 11: 7 Ways To Attract Happiness 45

Chapter 12: You're Good Enough 49

Chapter 13: 7 Signs You Have Found A Keeper 52

Chapter 14: 6 Ways On How To Get Over A Crush 56

Chapter 15: Happy People Spend Time Alone 59

Chapter 16: 7 Ways To Get The Partner You Want 62

Chapter 17: 6 Habits of Ridiculously Likeable People 66

Chapter 18: How to Love Yourself First 71

Chapter 19: Confidence: The Art of Humble-Pride 74

Chapter 20: This Is Life 76

Chapter 21: Happy People Find Reasons to Laugh and Forge Deep
Connections 79

Chapter 22: Deal With Your Fears Now 82

Chapter 23: 8 Signs You Have Found Your Soulmate 86

Chapter 24: It's Not Your Job to Tell Yourself "No" 91

Chapter 25: 6 Ways To Get People To Like You 94

Chapter 26: Nothing Is Impossible 98

Chapter 27: 10 Facts About Attraction 101

Chapter 28: Make Time for Your Partner 105

Chapter 29: 7 Ways On How To Attract Success In Life 107

Chapter 30: 7 Ways To Keep Your Relationship Fresh And Exciting
.... 111

Chapter 31: 7 Ways To Deal With Sexual Problems In a Relationship
.... 115

Chapter 1:

6 Tips To Find The One

Finding someone who matches our criteria can be a difficult task. We always look for a person who is a knight in shining armor. And by time, we make our type. We are finding someone who looks and behaves like our ideal one. We always fantasize about our right one. No matter how hard it may seem to find someone, we should never lose hope. Sharing is always beneficial. And if you trust someone enough to share your life with them, then it's worth the risk to be taken. The person you chose depends upon you only. The advice can only give you an idea, and you have to act on your own.

Now, when looking for someone from scratch can be difficult for many of us. That person can either be the wrong one or the right one. Only time can tell you that. But you both need to grow together to know if you can survive together. And if not, then separation is the only possible way. But if you find the right one, then it will all be good. You have to have faith in yourself. Be your wingman and go after whatever you desire.

1. Be Patient

When looking for someone you want to spend your time with, someone you want to dedicate a part of your life to, you have to devote your time looking for the one. Be patient with everyone you meet so you will get to know them better. They will be more open towards you when you give them time to open. Doing everything fast will leave you confused. Don't only talk with them. Notice their habits, share secrets and trust them. They will be more comfortable around you when they think that you are willing to cooperate.

2. Keep Your Expectations Neutral

When you find someone for you, they can either leave you disappointed or satisfied. That all depends on your expectations. If you wait for prince charming and get a knight, then you will be nothing but uncomfortable with them. Keep them neutral. Try to make sure that you get to know a person before passing your judgment.

3. Introduce Them To Your Friends

The people who love you tend to get along together. The first thing we do after finding a competitor is telling a friend. We usually go for the people our loved one has chosen for us. While finding the one is all you. They can play a part in giving advice, but they can't decide for you. When we see one, we want everyone to get to know them.

4. Don't Be Discouraged

You are 30 and still haven't found anyone worth your time. If so, then don't get discouraged. That love comes to us when we least expect it. You have to keep looking for that one person who will brighten your days and keep you happy. Please don't go looking for it. It will come to you itself and will make you happy.

5. Look Around You

Sometimes our journey of finding the one can be cut short when we see the one by our side—someone who has been our friend or someone who was with us all along. You will feel happier and more comfortable with finding the right person within your friend. It will make things much more manageable. And one day, you will realize that he was the one all this time. Sometimes we can find one in mutual friends. They may be strangers, but you know a little about them already. However, finding the one within your friend can save you a lot of trouble.

6. Keep The Sparks Fresh

Whatever happens, don't let your spark die because it will become the source of your compassion. It will make a path for you to walk on with your ideal one. Keep that passion, that love alive. If there is no spark, then you will live a life without any light. So, make your partner and yourself feel that compassion in your growth.

Conclusion

Finding one can be a difficult job, but once we find them, they can make us the happiest in the world. And if that person is honest with you, then there is nothing more you should need in one. You can always change your partner until you find the one because they are always their ones too. You have to focus on finding your own.

Chapter 2:

9 New Date Ideas That Will Deepen Your Relationship

When you commit to a relationship, you need to know your partner well. If you don't know your partner, then how do you expect your relationship to last? A date is something that someone plans for their partner. Dates usually involve doing something or going somewhere with your partner, and you find it fun, but sometimes everybody gets bored of the same cliché date ideas. Sometimes, these kinds of dates aren't enough to know your partner. Surely you want to deepen your bond with your partner. Here are some new date ideas to deepen your relationship.

1. Go For A Walk

We have often seen people go for a walk to clear their minds. Walking helps people think differently. It is not exactly an epic date idea, but it will remove both of your brains. It'll help you talk to each other. When you and your partner start talking more, your bond will automatically deepen. After the walk, you will feel very fresh, but you will also feel like you now know your partner more.

2. Read A Book Together

As a kid, we all loved to hear some bedtime stories, but we forgot how blissful it felt as we grew up. At night when both of you feel tired, then select a book you both like, lay down and read it to each other in turns.

3. Spa At Home

We all need some time to relax. You don't always have to go outside for a date, and you could give yourself a day off and bring out all the face, hair, and every other mask you have because this is a spa day, you could give each other massages and help the other relax. Also, don't forget the scented candles.

4. Plan Trips Together

Haven't we all dreamed about discovering the world but don't tell anyone, well what are you waiting for? Sit together and look through places you would want to visit even if you can't right now! Daydreaming isn't a sin.

5. Go For a Boat Ride

Have you watched tangled? If yes, you would surely want to experience that romantic scene on the boat; if you haven't still done it, what are you waiting for? Rent a boat, take your partner with you. It'll just be you, your partner, and the stars. You could set some slow music on your phone and enjoy that quality time with your partner.

6. Take A Step Out of Your Comfort Zone

Almost all of us have a fixed routine, but it is good to mess with your way once in a while. As a couple, you would have a place where you usually go for food, a cinema where you typically watch a movie, an ice cream parlor where you usually buy the ice cream from but isn't it all getting boring? This is the time to forget about your comfort zone and explore something else. Go to a new restaurant, a museum you haven't been to before together, or any other place you and your partner haven't visited yet.

7. Paint Together

Not all of us are good at painting, but what's stopping you from painting something together. It sounds fun, doesn't it? Just buy a few art supplies and a canvas and paint whatever you want to paint. Then hang it somewhere; it seems nice, it doesn't need to be an artistic masterpiece, but it'll bring back the memories of that fantastic day whenever you look at it.

8. Watch The Sunset Together

There are many places where you can see the sunset together, so find the home that feels perfect to you and take your partner there for a date and watch the sunset together along with your partner's favorite dish to eat. Not only will this bring a wide smile to your partner's face, but it'll also help you deepen your connection with them.

9. Meet At a Coffee Shop

At the start of a relationship, most people decide to meet at a coffee shop, but as time passes, they don't do it anymore, but why not? Decide a time and a coffee shop and meet up there. Drink coffee and eat something if you like. You will have fun with this typical date idea.

Conclusion:

These simple and fun ideas will help you deepen your relationship with your partner. Don't fret if you think you don't know your partner much because it is never too late. Just put in some effort, and your bond with your partner would be more profound than the ocean.

Chapter 3:

7 Ways To Live Together In Harmony With Your Partner

A harmonious relationship can make a person's life happy and beautiful, but, unfortunately, not all of us are blessed with a harmonious relationship. It is essential to work on your relationship in order to make it work. Creating a harmonious bond between you and your partner can make your relationship more healthy and stable. The dream relationship of everybody is to feel loved, accepted, and respected but to achieve such a relationship, and you need to first work on yourself. You need to make sure that you are doing your best at making your partner feel loved.

Most people nowadays want to find their soulmates, but even when they see their soulmates, they don't have a peaceful relationship; the lack of harmony causes this.

Here are 7 ways to live together in harmony with your partner.

1. Accept Your Partners the Way They Are

The first step to a harmonious relationship is acceptance. It would be best to accept your partners the way they are; distancing them from yourself because of a simple mistake can lead to a toxic relationship. If you choose to love a person and be with them, you need to accept the good and bad in them. As they say that no one is perfect, we all are a work in progress. When you cannot receive your partner the way they are, a harmonious relationship cannot be achieved. It would help if you allowed them to evolve and support them throughout this journey.

2. Be Gentle and Compassionate

When you embody gentleness and compassion, your relationship bond deepens, and there is harmony in the relationship. Instead of jumping to conclusions and reacting dramatically, you need to respond with gentleness and understand your partner's feelings.

Compassion brings grace to a person. To achieve a harmonious relationship, you should give your partner grace to work on themselves, understand, and give them space to evolve and mature. It may take time, but it strengthens a relationship.

3. Expectations Should Be Released

With expectations comes disappointment. Expectations are the unspoken standards you expected your partner to live up to. When your partner does not live up to your expectations, you might feel upset or disappointed, but how can you have such high expectations from your partner about things that are unspoken. Work on letting go of these ideals that the society and your subconscious mind created about how a relationship should be. Release the attachment to situations turning out a specific way. Brace yourself for different outcomes of different situations. Don't expect too much from your partner because your partner, like you, cannot always live up to your expectation.

4. Personal Space In A Relationship

Every human being needs personal space; we often see couples that are always together. It may feel exciting and comforting at first, but everyone needs their personal space to think and function properly. After being with each other with no personal space, one can start feeling suffocated and may behave negatively. It would help if you had time to breathe, to expand, and to look within. To evolve, you need space. Personal space between couples proves that their relationship is healthy and robust.

5. Honesty

Honest communication is not just a factor to achieve a harmonious relationship but also to have any relationship at all. Not being truthful can cause conflicts and problems in a relationship. Moreover, being a liar can be a toxic trait that can cause your partner to end the relationship. But before being honest with your partner, you need to be honest with yourself. Know your true self, explore the good and bad in yourself. Don't hide your mistakes from your partner; instead, be honest and apologize to them before it is too late. Honesty is a crucial factor in achieving a harmonious relationship.

6. Shun Your Ego

Ego and harmony cannot simply go hand in hand; where ego exists, harmony cannot be established. Often by some people, ego is considered a toxic trait. This is the ego that stops a person from apologizing for his mistakes, which can create tension among the couple. The stubbornness to do things your way is caused by ego and can easily result in unwanted scenarios. These are not the components of a healthy relationship. So to establish a harmonious relationship, you should remove ego and learn to compromise a bit. By removing ego, you allow yourself to be more flexible and understanding.

7. Let Go if Unnecessary Emotional Pain

When you keep hurting over old resentments, you convert that pain into toxic feelings that are not good for a relationship. These poisonous feelings can make you make some bad decisions that may result in your partner feeling unsafe around you. This pain can cause you to bury your positives feeling inside. As a result of this, you may feel pessimistic and may exaggerate minor conflicts into something more. A person must let go of this emotional stress and pain. You can let go by going to a therapist or yoga and meditation. Once you have let go of the pain, your heart is now open to a peaceful and harmonious relationship.

To establish a harmonious relationship, you have to accept and understand your partner and work on yourself. Also, work on your radical integrity.

Chapter 4:
7 Signs You're More Attractive Than You Think

We feel conscious about ourselves every now and then. We are our own biggest critics. Finding flaws in ourselves sometimes leads to constructive criticism, which in turn leads to self-development. But sometimes, the constructive criticism might lead to a self-destructive reproach that will disturb the healthy and happy life you're living. It's normal to have self-doubts, wondering how people see us or what they think about us.

We live in a society where there is constant pressure to look your best self. People might point out our flaws and weaknesses, but what matters is how we emerge from it all. A study by Feynman in 2007 revealed that the way people see us determines how they will treat us. So, it's best if we remain confident and comfortable in our skin. Our appearances can either make or break the first impression of how people will perceive us. Research in 2016 by Lammers, Davis, Davidson, and Hogue revealed that first impressions could have a lasting effect on our relationship with the other person.

Many of us are used to being hard on ourselves. So it practically seems like a joke that anyone would find us attractive. Here are 7 signs that will confirm that you're more attractive than you think!

1. You Rarely Get Compliments

I know many of you wouldn't believe this but just hear me out first. Have you ever put on your most fabulous outfit, put on that sexy cologne, and dressed up all stunning from head to toe? You were confident enough that all eyes would be on you, and you will receive tons of compliments. But by the end of it all, you have hardly received any! Naturally, this would lead to you having some severe self-doubts about yourself. But you needn't worry. Psychology says that whenever we see a gorgeous person, we assume that he/she might have very high self-esteem. As a result, people rarely compliment those people. People also think that you already know how stunning you look, and you might be getting a lot of attention already. So, they avoid complimenting you too much. Instead of treating the scarcity of compliments as a bad thing, just maybe you are already the subject of many secret admirers.

2. The Compliments You Get Feel Insincere

Finally, you're receiving those compliments that you have been waiting for, for so long. But to your surprise, they sound apathetic and emotionless. You're confirmed now that you don't come off quite as attractive to other people. But we have a theory on this too. Suppose there is a gorgeous friend of yours. Do you constantly flatter them and gush about their appearance? You don't. You only compliment them if they're wearing a new outfit or changed their looks. The same happens to you. People think you already know how beautiful you are, so they don't pay much attention to the compliments they give you. The sole reason why the compliments sound so mundane and trivial. So, if you have been experiencing this, then you're more attractive than you think.

3. **People Get Nervous Around You**

Whenever you enter a room, you notice people suddenly being all nervous around you. This may happen because they're caught off guard by how gorgeous you look. They may feel pressured to make an excellent first impression since you've already made a perfect one on them. As a result, they try to hide their flaws in In front of you. They might become either too confident or underconfident. People tend to become awkward and nervous when they see other people as too attractive or too perfect.

4. **You Find Yourself Locking Eyes with a Lot of People**

We, humans, tend to stare at the desirable things we want. Research by the University of Oslo in 2015 found that your brain gives you a dopamine shot when you look at something pleasurable. While it may not always be the case that people staring at you might find you attractive. Sometimes it can just be a mistake, or maybe you have worn your shirt wrong, or there's something stuck on your teeth, but a lot of times, we stare and lock eyes with the people we find good-looking. So, if a person keeps staring at you even if you have caught them and passes a smile, it definitely means he likes what he's staring at.

5. People Are Surprised by Your Insecurities

People might become shocked when you tell them about your complexes and insecurities. They think that since you're so gorgeous, you have nothing to worry about. But we all have our bad days where we go through self-doubts and low self-esteem. People wouldn't see this as such a problem because they would love to look like you and don't even notice the flaws you point out about yourself. Instead, they might become irritated when you complain about your issues because you look so self-confident and self-sufficient to them.

6. People Are Often Too Polite or Too Unfriendly To You

You find people being either too optimistic or too pessimistic around you. They either might be too warm and friendly or too harsh and rude when you first meet them. The truth is, people, tend to react strongly to the people they find attractive. Some people might find excuses to spend time with you and praise you, while others may sound too petty around you. This might also be because of the jealousy they may feel towards you. A positive person will always see you as an equal and will always treat you with a polite and friendly attitude.

7. People Are Interested In You

You might feel people asking a lot of questions about you and getting to know you better. They carry the conversation and like talking to you from time to time. Even though your communication skills are pretty average, they would still speak to you with the same interest. This is because they might think that you would have a great personality. After all, you have a pretty face. They would become compromising and would jump at the first opportunity to help you. We tend to be friendlier and more generous to the people subconsciously we find attractive. By helping you, they want to look good in your eyes too.

Conclusion

You need to look past your insecurities, embrace your flaws, and accept the characteristics that people value in you. Don't forget that in the end, a good heart always wins over good looks. Don't become a victim of societal pressure and mould yourself into a perfect and flawless human being. There is nothing more attractive than appreciating yourself with all the good and the bad and knowing your worth. Find happiness in being vulnerable and weak, through the tough and challenging times. Life is a roller coaster ride, so you shouldn't have a need to feel perfect all the time!

Chapter 5:
6 Ways To Attract Anything You Want In Life

It is common human nature that one wants whatever one desires in life. People work their ways to get what they need or want. This manifestation of wanting to attract things is almost in every person around us. A human should be determined to work towards his goal or dreams through sheer hard work and will. You have to work towards it step by step because no matter what we try or do, we will always have to work for it in the end. So, it is imperative to work towards your goal and accept the fact that you can't achieve it without patience and dedication.

We have to start by improving ourselves day by day. A slight change a day can help us make a more considerable change for the future. We should feel the need to make ourselves better in every aspect. If we stay the way we are, tomorrow, we will be scared of even a minor change. We feel scared to let go of our comfort zone and laziness. That way, either we or our body can adapt to the changes that make you better, that makes you attract better.

1. Start With Yourself First

We all know that every person is responsible for his own life. That is why people try to make everything revolves around them. It's no secret that everyone wants to associate with successful, healthy, and charming people. But, what about ourselves? We should also work on ourselves to become the person others would admire. That is the type of person people love. He can also easily attract positive things to himself. It becomes easier to be content with your desires. We need to get ourselves together and let go of all the things we wouldn't like others doing.

2. Have A Clear Idea of Your Wants

Keeping in mind our goal is an easy way to attract it. Keep reminding yourself of all the pending achievements and all the dreams. It helps you work towards it, and it enables you to attract whatever you want. Make sure that you are aware of your intentions and make them count in your lives. You should always make sure to have a crystal-clear idea of your mindset, so you will automatically work towards it. It's the most basic principle to start attracting things to you.

3. Satisfaction With Your Achievements

It is hard to stop wanting what you once desired with your heart, but you should always be satisfied with anything you are getting. This way, when you attract more, you become happier. So, it is one of the steps to draw things, be thankful. Be thankful for what you are getting and what you haven't. Every action has a reason for itself. It doesn't mean just to let it be. Work for your goals but also acknowledge the ones already achieved by you in life. That way you will always be happy and satisfied.

4. Remove Limitations and Obstacles

We often limit ourselves during work. We have to know that there is no limit to working for what you want when it comes to working for what you want. You remove the obstacles that are climbing their way to your path. It doesn't mean to overdo yourselves, but only to check your capability. That is how much pressure you can handle and how far you can go in one go. If you put your boundaries overwork, you will always do the same amount, thus, never improving further. Push yourself a little more each time you work for the things you want in life.

5. Make Your Actions Count

We all know that visualizing whatever you want makes it easier to get. But we still cannot ignore the fact that it will not reach us unless we do some hard work and action. Our actions speak louder than words, and they speak louder than our thoughts. So, we have to make sure that our actions are built of our brain image. That is the way you could attract the things you want in life. Action is an essential rule for attracting anything you want in life.

6. Be Optimistic About Yourselves

Positivity is an essential factor when it comes to working towards your goals or dreams. When you learn to be optimistic about almost everything, you will notice that everything will make you satisfied. You will attract positive things and people. Negative vibes will leave you disappointed in yourself and everyone around you. So, you will have to practice positivity. It may not be easy at first while everyone around you is pushing you to negativity. That is where your test begins, and you have to prove yourself to them and yourself. And before you know it, you are attracting things you want.

Conclusion

Everyone around us wants to attract what they desire, but you have to start with yourself first. You only have to focus on yourself to achieve what you want. And attracting things will come naturally to you. Make sure you work for your dreams and goals with all your dedication and determination. With these few elements, you will be attracting anything you want.

Chapter 6:

6 Habits of Strong Couples

Relationships don't always come with guaranteed success. They are always a risk for those who choose to fall in love with each other. People open themselves up to the possibilities of heartbreak and getting hurt whenever things don't go their way. They make so much effort and invest a considerable part of themselves into the relationship in the hopes of not getting emotionally betrayed in the end. Relationships can be stressful and difficult to bear, and the couple's habits can have a powerful impact on the relationship. We can either create positive or negative habits, but once we start practicing them, they will eventually become a part of our unconscious act.

Research says that it takes us 21 days to develop a habit, whether positive or negative. When it comes to having a healthy and happy relationship, certain habits can have a positive and powerful impact. Here are some healthy habits that you need to practice every day to become second nature to you and help you build a stronger connection with your partner.

1. Always Show Mutual Respect

Respecting your partner is a crucial ingredient for creating a healthy, happy, and long-lasting connection. It is a habit that is worth developing. Expressing respect towards your partner shows your love, acceptance, and warmth towards them. It shows that you value your partner, no matter the differences. Even if you both have a different outlook on life, you mustn't disrespect your partner or put them down. This goes both ways. If your partner disagrees with you, they should show respect towards you. It's not about both of you not agreeing on a situation, but rather how you handle the issue as a team that makes all the difference in the world.

2. Communicate With Each Other

Communication is perhaps an essential quality of a healthy relationship. But there are instances when we can't communicate appropriately with our partners or come off as emotionally unavailable to them. But healthy and happy couples have this game down. They vocalize their feelings and love for each other and offer compliments and gestures. And instead of sweeping the issues under the rug, they discuss all the bad and negative stuff that bothers them. No matter how awkward or uncomfortable you both might feel, it's always essential to talk about your feelings to move forward and grow.

3. Spending Some Time Apart

As much as it is vital to spend time together with your partner, it's equally important to spend it apart. Being able to be independent and doing your stuff is critical in any relationship. You cannot always depend on your partner for things that you can easily do yourself. Spending too much time together can create unhealthy codependency. Both of them should maintain healthy boundaries and autonomy to ensure a long-lasting relationship.

4. Love Languages

Gary Chapman came up with the concept that men and women have five love languages. They can either be words of affirmation, receiving gifts, quality time, acts of service, and physical touch. You and your partner need to know which love language suits you both the best. It will help both of you feel loved and stay connected with each other. Furthermore, you must attend to your partner's love language constantly.

5. Appreciate Each Other

We often forget to let our partners know that we appreciate them and don't show them much affection and appreciation. We might have it in our mind, but we fail to express and deliver it to them. But it's always important to show your significant other how much you love and appreciate them and their efforts. This could also be done through words, cards, flowers, acts of kindness, and more.

6. Say Sorry and Mean It

Partners step on each other's toes all the time, whether in big or small ways. It might be a disagreement, argument, or a fight, but recognizing your role in your partner's pain is essential. No matter who is at fault, both of you should aim for an apology that expresses empathy, takes responsibility for your wrongdoings, and shows that you're striving to change your behavior.

Conclusion

Relationships always require time, patience, and love but also healthy habits. It's easier to fall for someone and promise them the world. But if you want to make your relationship long-lasting, efforts are always required. Sometimes, the proper habits are all we need to make what we have with our partners.

Chapter 7:

8 Ways To Love Yourself First

"Your task is not to seek for love, but merely to seek and find all the barriers within yourself that you have built against it." - Rumi.

Most of us are so busy waiting for someone to come into our lives and love us that we have forgotten about the one person we need to love the most – ourselves. Most psychologists agree that being loved and being able to love is crucial to our happiness. As quoted by Sigmund Freud, "love and work ... work and love. That's all there is." It is the mere relationship of us with ourselves that sets the foundation for all other relationships and reveals if we will have a healthy relationship or a toxic one.

Here are some tips on loving yourself first before searching for any kind of love in your life.

1. Know That Self-Love Is Beautiful

Don't ever consider self-love as being narcissistic or selfish, and these are two completely different things. Self-love is rather having positive regard for our wellbeing and happiness. When we adopt self-love, we see higher levels of self-esteem within ourselves, are less critical and harsh with ourselves while making mistakes, and can celebrate our positive qualities and accept all our negative ones.

2. Always Be Kind To Yourself

We are humans, and humans are tended to get subjected to hurts, shortcomings, and emotional pain. Even if our family, friends, or even our partners may berate us about our inadequacies, we must learn to accept ourselves with all our imperfections and flaws. We look for acceptance from others and be harsh on ourselves if they tend to be cruel or heartless with us. We should always focus on our many positive qualities, strengths, and abilities, and admirable traits; rather than harsh judgments, comparisons, and self-hatred get to us. Always be gentle with yourself.

3. Be the Love You Feel Within Yourself

You may experience both self-love and self-hatred over time. But it would be best if you always tried to focus on self-love more. Try loving yourself and having positive affirmations. Do a love-kindness meditation or spiritual practices to nourish your soul, and it will help you feel love and compassion toward yourself. Try to be in that place of love throughout your day and infuse this love with whatever interaction you have with others.

4. Give Yourself A Break

We don't constantly live in a good phase. No one is perfect, including ourselves. It's okay to not be at the top of your game every day, or be happy all the time, or love yourself always, or live without pain. Excuse your bad days and embrace all your imperfections and mistakes. Accept your negative emotions but don't let them overwhelm you. Don't set high standards for yourself, both emotionally and mentally. Don't judge yourself for whatever you feel, and always embrace your emotions wholeheartedly.

5. Embrace Yourself

Are you content to sit all alone because the feelings of anxiety, fear, guilt, or judgment will overwhelm you? Then you have to practice being comfortable in your skin. Go within and seek solace in yourself, practice moments of alone time and observe how you treat yourself. Allow yourself to be mindful of your beliefs, feelings, and thoughts, and embrace solitude. The process of loving yourself starts with understanding your true nature.

6. Be Grateful

Rhonda Bryne, the author of The Magic, advises, "When you are grateful for the things you have, no matter how small they may be, you will see those things instantly increase." Look around you and see all the things that you are blessed to have. Practice gratitude daily and be thankful for all the things, no matter how good or bad they are. You will immediately start loving yourself once you realize how much you have to be grateful for.

7. Be helpful To Those Around You

You open the door for divine love the moment you decide to be kind and compassionate toward others. "I slept and dreamt that life was a joy. I awoke and saw that life was service. I acted, and behold, and service was a joy." - Rabindranath Tagore. The love and positive vibes that you wish upon others and send out to others will always find a way back to you. Your soul tends to rejoice when you are kind, considerate, and compassionate. You have achieved the highest form of self-love when you decide to serve others. By helping others, you will realize that you don't need someone else to feel complete; you are complete. It will help you feel more love and fulfilment in your life.

8. Do Things You Enjoy Doing

If you find yourself stuck in a monotonous loop, try to get some time out for yourself and do the things that you love. There must be a lot of hobbies and passions that you might have put a brake on. Dust them off and start doing them again. Whether it's playing any sport, learning a new skill, reading a new book, writing in on your journal, or simply cooking or baking for yourself, start doing it again. We shouldn't compromise on the things that make us feel alive. Doing the things we enjoy always makes us feel better about ourselves and boost our confidence.

Conclusion:

Loving yourself is nothing short of a challenge. It is crucial for your emotional health and ability to reach your best potential. But the good news is, we all have it within us to believe in ourselves and live the best life we possibly can. Find what you are passionate about, appreciate yourself, and be grateful for what's in your life. Accept yourself as it is.

Chapter 8:

8 Signs Someone Misses You

Missing someone can be very painful, almost as if there is something incomplete about your life. You think about them all the time, and the more you try not to think of them, the more you end up doing that. You might find your thoughts wandering and can't seem to focus on anything other than them. You may either find comfort in binge eating or constantly go through their stuff. Well, you're not the only one who might be going through this torture. What if someone is experiencing the same stuff but for you? Here are some signs that tell you someone is missing you.

1. They Keep Track of Your Social Media

If they haven't unfriended, unfollowed, or blocked you yet, the chances are that they are still keeping track of you. If you find them constantly reacting to your stories, or liking your pictures the minute you put them up, then they're visiting your profile again and again. They have kept their slot open for making a conversation or giving you a hint to try to make conversation with them.

2. Did They Find Your Replacement Yet?

For someone ready to move on, it takes a second to find a replacement. If they haven't found one yet, the chances are that they are still reminiscing over you. They're hoping that you'll reconnect and thus, still pine after you. Even if they're hooking up with someone as a rebound, chances are they're doing everything in their power to forget you but are failing miserably.

3. They Reach Out To You Randomly

Receiving those drunk late-night texts/calls? They're miserable, and all they want to do is talk to you. If they were out there having the time of their life, they wouldn't even remember you let alone bother to text or call you. If they do, it's obviously because you're on their mind and alcohol just gave them a head start to get in touch with you again.

4. Rousing Your Jealousy So You Would Notice Them

Have they suddenly started posting a lot about their new life on social media? Chances are they're most certainly trying hard to make you sit up and take notice of them. If they're hanging out with a lot of people that you've never seen or heard of and having a fantastic time, then they're trying to make you jealous.

5. They Throw Shade At You

If they're making snide comments or remarks about you or a new partner, they're still clearly hurt and miss you. They might pass a statement on your outfit or your appearance and lash out at you, trying to make you feel as bad as they do. They may also show disapproval of your new date and point out negative things about them. It's clear that they still haven't moved on and clung to that thin thread of hope.

6. They Do Things To Get Your Attention

Do they post stuff that points towards you? Or do they write cute love letters or poems mentioning you? This is a pretty obvious sign that they miss you and want to get back in their life. They might also ask your friends about you and crash those uninvited parties because they want to see you. You might also see them around more than usual.

7. They Hoard Your Stuff

Are they still keeping your shirt/hoodie and making excuses not to give it even when you have asked them a million times? Or are they keeping even the most useless thing that you might have given them years ago? It's probably because they go through this stuff and relive all the old memories associated with them. They're still not ready to give them up and move on.

8. From The Horse's Mouth:

The most obvious and straightforward sign that someone misses you? They tell you themself! Some people don't like to play games and do unnecessary things to gain your attention or throw hints and clues at you and wait for you to notice them. They tell you straight away that they miss you and they want to do something about it.

Conclusion:

Now that you have all the signs on your plate, it's up to you whether you want to give them a second chance or move on from all of this. The choice is yours!

Chapter 9:

6 Signs You Have A Fear of Intimacy

Intimacy avoidance or avoidance anxiety, also sometimes referred to as the fear of intimacy, is characterized as the fear of sharing a close emotional or physical relationship with someone. People who experience it do not consciously want to avoid intimacy; they even long for closeness, but they frequently push others away and may even sabotage relationships for many reasons.

The fear of intimacy is separate from the fear of vulnerability, though both of them can be closely intertwined. A person who has a fear of intimacy may be comfortable becoming vulnerable and showing their true self to their trusted friends and relatives. This problem often begins when a person finds relationships becoming too close or intimate. Fear of intimacy can stem from several causes. Overcoming this fear and anxiety can take time, but you can work on it if you know the signs of why you have the fear in the first place.

1. Fear Of Commitment

A person who has a fear of intimacy can interact well with others initially. It's when the relationship and its value grow closer that everything starts to fall apart. Instead of connecting with your partner on an intimate level, you find ways and excuses to end the relationship and replace it with yet another superficial relationship. Some might even call you a 'serial dater,' as you tend to lose interest after a few dates and abruptly end the relationship. The pattern of emerging short-term relationships and having a 'commitment phobia' can signify that you fear intimacy.

2. Perfectionism

The idea of erfectionism often works to push others away rather than draw them near. The underlying fear of intimacy often lies in a person who thinks he does not deserve to be loved and supported. The constant need for someone to prove themself to be perfect and lovable can cause people to drift apart from them. Absolute perfectionism lies in being imperfect. We should be able to accept the flaws of others and should expect them to do the same for us. There's no beauty in trying to be perfect when we know we cannot achieve it.

3. Difficulty Expressing Needs

A person who has a fear of intimacy may have significant difficulty in expressing needs and wishes. This may stem from feeling undeserving of another's support. You need to understand that people cannot simply 'mind read,' they cannot know your needs by just looking at you; this might cause you to think that your needs go unfulfilled and your feelings of unworthiness are confirmed. This can lead to a vicious cycle of you not being vocal about your needs and lacking trust in your partner, and your relationship is meant to doom sooner or later.

4. Sabotaging Relationships

People who have a fear of intimacy may sabotage their relationship in many ways. You might get insecure, act suspicious, and accuse your partner of something that hasn't actually occurred. It can also take the form of nitpicking and being very critical of a partner. Your trust in your partner would lack day by day, and you would find yourself drifting apart from them.

5. Difficulties with Physical Contact

Fear of intimacy can lead to extremes when it comes to physical contact. It would swing between having a constant need for physical contact or avoiding it entirely. You might be inattentive to your partner's needs and solely concentrate on your own need for sexual release or gratification. People with a fear of intimacy may also recoil from sex altogether. Both ends of the spectrum lead to an inability to let go or communicate intimately emotionally. Letting yourself be emotionally naked and bringing up your fears and insecurities to your partner may help you overcome this problem.

6. You're Angry - A Lot

One way that the deep, subconscious fear of intimacy can manifest is via anger. Constant explosions of anger might indicate immaturity, and immature people are not able to form intimate relationships. Everyone gets angry sometimes, and it's an emotion that we cannot ignore, even if we want to. But if you find that your feelings of anger bubble up constantly or inappropriately, a fear of intimacy may be lurking underneath. Don't deny these intimacy issues, but instead put them on the table and communicate effectively with the person you are interested in.

Conclusion

Actions that root out in fear of intimacy only perpetuate the concern. With effort, especially a good therapist, many people have overcome this fear and developed the understanding and tools needed to create a long-term intimate relationship.

Chapter 10:

6 Ways To Flirt With Someone

No matter how confident and bold we assume ourselves to be, we tend to freeze up and utter a wimpy 'hey' when we see our crush approaching us. Flirting doesn't always come easily to everyone, and there's always struggle, awkwardness, and shyness that follows. But, some people are natural-born flirters and just get the dating thing right.

Knowing how to flirt and actually showing someone that you're interested in them sexually or romantically can be a minefield. But once you get your hands on it, you'll probably become an expert in no time. If you struggle with flirting, we've got some tips to help you master the art of flirting and getting your crush's attention. Below are some ways to flirt with someone successfully.

Be Confident But Mysterious

There's nothing sexier than someone who has a lot of confidence. Of course, I'm not talking about being too overconfident, and it will tend to push people away from you. But if you're strutting down the halls as you own them, your crush (and everyone else) will notice you. Don't give away too much of yourself while being confident. People tend to get intrigued by someone who gives off mysterious vibes. They show their interest in you and avail every opportunity to try to get to know you better. This will lead to you having a chance to make up a good conversation with your crush and even flirt with them in between.

Show That You're Interested In Their Life

Who doesn't love compliments and talking about themselves all the time? We come along with people who mostly like to talk than to listen. If you get a chance to talk to your crush, don't waste it. Ask them questions about their life, get to know their views and ideas about certain things like politics, fashion, controversies, show that you're genuinely interested in them. They will love your curious nature and would definitely look forward to having another conversation with you. This will also give your brownie points of getting to know them better.

Greet Them Whenever You Pass Them

Seeing your crush approach you or simply seeing them standing in the halls can be the scariest feeling ever. You will probably follow your gut reaction and become nervous; either you'll walk past them hurriedly or look down at your phone and pretend like you're in the middle of a text conversation battle. But you have to ignore those instincts, and you have to look up at them and simply smile. You don't have to indulge yourself in an extensive conversation with them. Just taking a second to wave or say hi can be more than enough to get yourself on your crush's radar, as you will come off as polite to them.

Make Ever-So-Slight Contact

The sexiest touches are often those electric ones that come unexpectedly, not the intentional ones that might make someone uncomfortable. Unnecessary touches can be a turn-on because they signal a willingness to venture beyond the safe boundaries that we usually maintain between ourselves and others. But be careful not to barge into them accidentally. Small, barely-there touches that only the two of you notice are the best. Let your foot slightly touch theirs or lightly brush past them.

Compliment Them

While everyone loves receiving compliments, try not to go overboard, or they would be more likely to squirm in their seat rather than ask you out. You should compliment them lightly about their outfit or fragrance or their features or personality, but keep the subtle flirtation for when the time and moment is right. Giving them compliments would make them think that you're interested in them and want to step up the equation with them.

Look At Them

Experts suggest that we look and then look away three times to get someone's attention. According to the Social Issues Research Centre, maintaining too much eye contact while flirting is people's most common mistake. Our eyes make a zigzag motion when we meet someone new - we look at them from eye to eye and then the nose. With friends, we look below their eye level to include the nose and mouth. The subtle flirt then widens that triangle to incorporate parts of the body. Please don't stare at someone too intensely, or else you'll end up making them feel uncomfortable.

Conclusion

It might seem nerve-wracking to put yourself out there and start flirting, but fear not! It's normal to get nervous around someone whom you like. Follow the above ways to seem confident and pull off a successful flirtation. Know the importance of keeping a balance between revealing your feelings and keeping the person you like intrigued.

Chapter 11:
7 Ways To Attract Happiness

We have seen a lot of people defining success as to their best of knowledge. While happiness is subjective from person to person, there's a law of attraction that remains constant for everyone in the world. It states that you will indirectly start to attract all the good things in life when you become happier. This is why happy people often have good lives where everything just somehow tends to work for them. Happiness not only feels good but can also make our manifestation attempts twice as effective. We shouldn't measure our happiness from external factors but instead, as cliche as it may sound, we should know that true happiness comes from the inside.

Here are some ways for you to attract happiness:

1. Make A Choice To Be Happy

When you choose to be as happy as you can in every moment of your life, your subconscious mind will start acknowledging your decision, and it will begin to find ways to bring more joy into your life. When you work towards your decision of being happy, the universe also plays its part and makes sure it attracts more situations in your life that you can be pleased about. The positive vibrations that you will give out will find their way back to you. You don't have to make the decision of being happy right away, as some of you might be going through a tough time. Sit, relax, and take some time to reflect on yourself first and then make a choice whenever you're ready.

2. Define What Happiness Means To You

We have also found ourselves asking this question a million times, "what exactly is happiness?" Some people would attach the idea of happiness with materialistic things such as a big house, expensive cars, branded clothes and shoes, designer bags, the latest technologies, and so forth. While for some, happiness is merely spending time with family and friends, doing the things that they love, and finding inner peace and calm.

3. React Positively Under All Situations

We could experience a thousand good things but a million bad ones in our everyday lives. And sometimes, it could be complicated for us to encounter any kind of happiness given the circumstances. Although these circumstances cannot be in our control, how we react to them is always in our hands. As our favorite Professor Dumbledore once said, "Happiness can be found even in the darkest of times if only one remembers to turn on the light." Similarly, we should always try to find that silver lining at the end of the dark tunnel, always seek some positivity in every situation. But we are only humans. Don't try to enforce positivity on yourself if you don't feel like it. It's okay to address all our emotions equally till you be yourself again.

4. Do Not Procrastinate

You might find it a bit weird, but procrastination does snatch your happiness away. No matter how much things are going well in your life, you would always find a loophole, a reason to be unhappy and dissatisfy with yourself a well as your life. Procrastination makes you believe that you are not living up to your fullest potential. You will get this nagging feeling that will eventually morph into negative emotions that would nearly eat you. So, try to avoid procrastination as much as possible and start doing the things that actually matter.

5. Stay Present

The key to becoming more focused, more at peace, more effective in manifesting, and eventually, much happier is to just live in the moment. Whatever you're doing in the present, try to be completely aware and focused on it. It will help you avoid all the negative feelings you have conjured up about the past and future. Try to stay present as much as you can; over time, it will become a habit, and you will develop the capability to face it all. This will definitely help you attract more happiness into your life.

6. Do Not Compare Yourself

As Theodore Rosevelt once said, "Comparison is the thief of joy." Whenever we compare ourselves to others, we tend to become ungrateful and strip ourselves of the ability to appreciate the good and abundance in our lives. We start to magnify the good in other people's lives and the bad that is in our own. We must understand that everyone is going through their own pace, and they all are secretly struggling with one thing or the other.

7. Don't Try Too Hard

Happiness demands patience. It is better to get into it gradually rather than being overeager. Many people take the law of attraction and being positive a little too far and start obsessing over it. They tend to panic if they get negative thoughts or are unable to attract the things they want. Don't get frustrated if things don't work out your way, and don't give up on the idea of happiness if you feel distressed. Try to prioritize your happiness and give others a reason to be happy too. Make yours as well as other's lives easy.

Conclusion:

Not many people know that, but being happy is actually the foundation towards attracting all your dreams and goals. When you adopt the habit of becoming truly happy every day, everything good will naturally follow you. Over time, happiness can even become your default state. Try your best to follow the guidelines above, and I guarantee that you will start feeling happier immediately.

Chapter 12:

You're Good Enough

People come and say 'I did something stupid today. I am so bad at this. Why is it always me?' You will acknowledge even if no one else says it, we often say it to ourselves.

So what if we did something stupid or somewhat a little awkward. I am sure no one tries to do such things voluntarily. Things happen and sometimes we cause them because we have a tendency to go out of our way sometimes. Or sometimes our ways have a possibility of making things strange.

It doesn't make you look stupid or dumb or ugly or less competent. These are the things you make up of yourself. I am not saying people don't judge. They do. But their judgment should not make you think less of yourself.

No matter how much you slip up, you must not stop and you must not bow down to some critique. You only have to be a little determined and content with yourself that you have got it alright.

You need to realize your true potential because no matter what anyone says, you have what it takes to get to the top.

Need some proof? Ask yourself, have you had a full belly today? Have you had a good night's sleep last night? Have you had the will and energy to get up and appear for your job and duties? Have you had the guts to ask someone out to dinner because you had a crush on them?

If you have a good answer to any of these questions, and you have done it all on your own with your efforts. Congratulations my friend, you are ready to appraise yourself.

You have now come to terms with your abilities and you don't need anyone else's approval or appraisal. You don't depend on anyone either psychologically or emotionally.

So now when the times get tough you can remind yourself that you went through it before. And even if you failed back then, you have the right energy and right state of mind to get on top of it now. You are now well equipped to get ahead of things and be a better person than you were the last time.

You are enough for everything good or not so good happening in and around you.

Your health, your relations, your carrier, your future. Everything can be good and better when you have straightened out your relationship with yourself. When you have found ways to talk to yourself ad make yourself realize your true importance. When you learn to admire yourself.

Once you learn to be your best critic, you can achieve anything. Without ever second-guessing yourself and ever trying to care for what anyone else will think.

If you find yourself in a position where you had your heart broken but you still kept it open, you should have a smile on your face. Because now you might be on your path to becoming a superior human being.

Chapter 13:

7 Signs You Have Found A Keeper

Are you looking for Mr. or Mrs. Right? Or do you think you have found the right person, but how can you be sure? Sometimes, we meet someone who seems like the person you would want to spend your whole life with, but during those times, someone is in for a quick hookup. The only partners worth keeping are the ones that give you the positive vibes that you need after a dull and tedious day, the ones that make you feel happy, and your relationship doesn't feel boring at all. Here are signs that you have found a keeper.

1. They Inspire You To Become A Better Person

When we meet someone very kind, helpful and overall a friendly person that person usually inspires us to be better and luckily the world is full of friendly people. Is your partner like this too? Is he warm, kind, and helpful? Does he inspire you to become a better version of yourself? Then you know you have found yourself a keeper. You know you have found the right person when your partner works hard, gives you and his family time, and has his life organized.

2. They Are Always There

There are times when we all suffer when things get tough to handle. At times like these, a person always needs support and love to get through the hard times. If your partner is there for you even when you can't defend yourself and they cheer you up, you know that this is a keeper. A perfect partner is someone who knows how to make you laugh even when you are crying, your partner will never believe the things people talk about behind your back, and he would never hesitate to lend you a hand when you need some help.

3. They Know You More Than Yourself

Sometimes it fascinates us how someone can know us more than we know ourselves; it feels perfect when someone knows how or what we are thinking. If your partner knows what you are feeling without telling them, then they are the one. Does your partner know what you are comfortable with? Can they tell when you feel upset? Do they motivate you to do better and ask you to chase after your dreams? If so, then don't waste more time thinking if this is the right person for you because it is.

4. Your Interests Are Common

Sure, opposites attract, but too many differences are not usually suitable for someone's relationship. It would help if you had a common interest with your partner, like having common beliefs, values, and religious perspectives. When you agree on these things, your bond will become more robust, and you would find it very easy to live with that person.

5. They Are Honest With You

Finding an honest person is a tiring thing to do; many people lie more than twice a day, but how can that affect your relationship? The right one may lie about small things that don't matter that much, like whether the color suits you or not; they may say those things to make you feel good about yourself, but lying about other things like financial status, health, or fidelity can be more serious. A true keeper would never keep these things from you, and they would always be honest with you even if the truth upsets you.

6. They Don't Feel Tired Of You

Although everyone needs some space, even from the person they love the most, he will never get tired of you if he is the one. Your partner will never feel bored with you; on the contrary, your partner will never get tired of looking at you, admiring you, being with you, and above all, love you. When a person is so in love with you that they want to spend every second of their life with you, then you know you have found a keeper.

7. You Are A Part Of Their Dreams

Can your partner not even imagine your life without you? Has your partner already planned his future, and you are a big part of it? If so, you know that this one's a keeper. You both have reached a point in your lives where even thinking about living without each other sounds absurd, and then you know that you have found a keeper.

Conclusion

A keeper is someone that loves, cherishes, and cares for you like no one has ever had. Don't worry if you haven't found your keeper, and it is just a matter of time before you do because, for every one of us, there is someone out there.

Chapter 14:

6 Ways On How To Get Over A Crush

At the time, having a crush might feel like the best feeling in the whole world. It makes you feel mature and young at the same time. When we see someone we like and get butterflies fluttering in our stomach, that is not without any reason. It might be because you have a crush on them. It can either be a slight go-to crush. The one where you like the person and get over them as soon as you find someone new. Or a big crush on someone, where you get stuck on a person for a reasonable amount of time. Usually, it's tough to get over a crush.

No matter how ecstatic someone would feel while crushing on someone, we someday have to get over it. It's a healthy way to lead a life. A crush should have to be gotten over within time. That feeling of wondrousness is limited and has to go someday. It may take a lot of time to get over it. But with the right amount of work and the right amount of feelings, we can get over a crush with no difficulty. Listed below are some ways to get over a crush.

1. Welcome Your Emotions

When you have a crush on someone, the best thing you can do to make things easier is accept these feelings and emotions. Telling yourself constantly that you don't like them will only add up to your problems. Accept the fact that you want someone and have a crush on them. It's pretty standard for a person to have a crush on someone. So, naturally, it's normal for you too. It will help you move on from them much easier if you have already accepted the feelings about them.

2. Take Your Time

You can't overcome a crush in one day. Even though it takes work and confusing emotions, it also takes a lot of time. Be patient while getting over an infatuation. If it is just a crush, then you will someday get over it. Don't rush things, and it will only confuse you with your feelings and get mixed signals from you. It will just be a matter of a week or month. Then you will be fresh and happy again.

3. Busy Yourself

When you sit by yourself all day, your mind will automatically go towards thinking about your crush. You will get the time to fantasize about them. This way, it will be much harder to get over someone. It would be best to keep yourself busy in your daily routine to avoid letting your feelings consume you. When you don't get the time to think about them, you will eventually get habitual of not remembering them daily. And slowly, you won't even notice, and you will completely forget them.

4. Talk With A Friend

Talking with someone familiar with the situation and someone who you trust fully can help a lot. A friend is needed in this situation sometimes. You can always talk to them about getting over your crush. They will help you get over them and will also help you go through the emotional pain. It's common to have mixed and confusing emotions at this time, so talking with someone who has a clear mind will let you understand the circumstances.

5. Try Meeting With New People

The easiest way to get over a crush is by meeting new people. Try to meet someone who might replace that crush for good. They might make you feel good about letting go of that part of your life gladly, as a desire can be pretty brutal. It would be best to make sure that the new person in you is there for a genuine relationship and not only to serve a purpose.

6. Know Your Worth

Running after someone who doesn't even return your feelings is not worth your time and energy. When you know that you deserve better than this, you will eventually get over a crush. They won't even have the idea of the struggle you put up to meet them. They will take you just as another person in their life. So, be it. Identify your worth and get over it.

Conclusion:

Getting over a crush can be pretty tricky for us, but we need to get over them at the right time. Don't work yourself out while doing so. It's normal to have a crush, and you will have much more in the future too. Just don't let it consume you.

Chapter 15:

Happy People Spend Time Alone

No man is an island except for similarly as we blossom with human contact and connections, so too would we be able to prosper from time burned through alone. Also, this, maybe, turns out to be particularly important right now since we're all in detachment. We've since quite a while ago slandered the individuals who decide to be distant from everyone else, except isolation shouldn't be mistaken for forlornness. Here are two mental reasons why investing energy in isolation makes us more joyful and more satisfied:

1. Spending Time Alone Reconnects Us

Our inclination for isolation might be transformative, as indicated by an examination distributed in the British Journal of Psychology in 2016. Utilizing what they call "the Savannah hypothesis of satisfaction," transformative clinicians Satoshi Kanazawa of the London School of Economics and Norman Li of Singapore Management University accept that the single, tracker accumulate way of life of our precursors structure the establishment of what satisfies us in present-day times. The group examined a study of 15,000 individuals matured somewhere between 18 and 28 in the United States. They found that individuals living in more thickly populated regions were fundamentally less cheerful than the individuals who lived in more modest networks.

"The higher the populace thickness of the prompt climate, the less glad" respondents were. The scientists accept this is because we had advanced mentally from when mankind, for the most part, existed on distant, open savannahs. Since quite a while ago, we have instilled an inclination to be content alone, albeit current life generally neutralizes that. Also, as good to beat all, they tracked down that the more clever an individual was, the more they appreciated investing energy alone. Along these lines, isolation makes you more joyful AND is evidence of your smarts. We're in.

2. Spending Time Alone Teaches Us Empathy

Investing in a specific measure of energy alone can create more compassion towards others than a milestone concentrate from Harvard. Scientists found that when enormous gatherings of individuals encircle us, it's harder for us to acquire viewpoints and tune into the sensations of others. However, when we venture outside that unique circumstance, the extra headspace implies we can feel for the situation of individuals around us in a more genuine and significant manner. Furthermore, that is uplifting news for others, but different investigations show that compassion and helping other people are significant to prosperity and individual satisfaction.

"At the point when you invest energy with a specific friend network or your colleagues, you foster a 'we versus them' attitude," clarifies psychotherapist and creator Amy Morin. "Investing energy alone assists you with growing more empathy for individuals who may not find a way into your 'inward circle.' "On the off chance that you're not used to isolation, it can feel awkward from the outset," she adds. "However, making that tranquil time for yourself could be critical to turning into the best form of yourself."

Chapter 16:
7 Ways To Get The Partner You Want

Love is that magical, indescribable feeling that makes us feel alive. It's a weird mix of both science and intuition, the one we won't get if we don't experience it by ourselves. Some people are better at finding 'The One' for themselves. Call it luck or good stalking skills, whatever floats your boat. While others, called the broken pickers, may struggle to find the perfect partner for them. The author of the famous book 'The Neighbour Next Door,' Grace Wabuke Klein, says, "Waiting doesn't have to mean pining, panicking, or desperately seeking. So often, we rush into the arms of just anyone. Instead, it's best to find someone who has our best interests in mind, sees the greatness in us and truly champions us."

Here are 6 tips to help you in getting the partner that you desire:

1. Make An Excellent First Impression

You have probably heard this phrase a million times, 'The first impression is the last impression,' and trust me, I cannot stress on this fact enough that you have to try to make the best first impression on them as possible. Researchers have found that people make up their mind in the first thirty seconds of meeting with others if they want to see them again or spend more time with them, or simply say goodbye to them. Going that extra mile to present yourself in the best light possible, walk confidently, talk confidently, be so full of confidence that it becomes guaranteed to impress the other person. Pastor Robert says, "The confidence that comes from becoming you is beautiful. But it shouldn't have even a hint of desperation in it."

2. Strive To Be More Attractive

Attraction is the most crucial aspect of a romantic relationship - the one that plays a massive role in deciding what type of partner we're willing to spend the rest of our lives with. The roles of love and attraction go hand in hand, according to tons of psychological studies. If you're attracted to someone and want them in your life, or if you're willing to be attractive to that special someone, then you're at the right place.

3. Try the Chameleon Effect

You might have heard about the Chameleon Effect here and there. But if you don't remember it, I am here to refresh your memory. When you're trying to get someone to fall in love with you, you start to copy their body movements, mannerisms and look for subtle cues. They will subconsciously begin to see you as an attractive, likable person. This is called the Chameleon Effect, which is proved to be useful in many circumstances. But beware! Don't make it too obvious or copy everything they do. It'll start making them feel weirded out, or they might see it as you making fun of them or teasing them, which could backfire on you if they take it the wrong way.

4. Tell Them Your Secrets and Ask Them About Theirs

If you have a sense of trust, affection, and shared values with the person you like, then you might think about opening up to them. There's nothing more intimate than being vulnerable and confessing something deep and personal to the person you want your partner to be. This will give him a boost of confidence that you trust him with your secrets, and he might think about doing the same with you. As opposed to small talk, personal questions and secrets hold a higher value of attraction. As a result, you both will come closer and won't hesitate to share your lives' experiences. The pull and interest would make that you both would feel towards each other.

5. Be Your Authentic Self Around Them

There's nothing sexier than being and showing the real you to the world, including the one you like. Showing your flaws and imperfections to the other person only makes them more attracted to you. Having a good sense of humour and making them laugh will warm them up to you faster and may even make them fall for you. Don't become shy and quiet or reserved and nervous when around them. Relax, take a deep breath, and show your exceptional qualities to make them realize what they're missing on. Studies have shown that people with high moral values are actually considered less attractive than those with a great sense of humour.

6. Make Friends With Their Friends

If you get along with their friends, then you may have a higher chance of getting them. As the spice girls once suggested, "If you wanna be my lover, you gotta get with my friends." If you both have the same group of friends, then boom! You got way too lucky. Psychologists have a triadic closure phenomenon to study the effect of people becoming more interested in you when you know their friends or a similar group. I'll give you an example; suppose you got a request from a random person on social media. The chances of you deleting that request are much higher than if you get a request from a person with who you have mutual friends.

7. Make Them Feel Special

The best way to get someone to do something for you is by giving them the desire of importance. Make them feel important by giving them affection and making small meaningful gestures that will make them feel unique and worthy. Remind them of their place in your life. Compliment them, make their favorite food, send them notes, spend time together, plan movie nights and dates, text them throughout the day that will show that they've crossed your mind. But don't become too clingy as it would annoy them. Just keep it simple and sweet.

Conclusion

Asking yourself about the kind of partner you want to attract is crucial, but it is one of the most critical questions that could become a gateway to achieving the type of love you want in your life. Keep a positive attitude, and work towards getting the person that you like. We all have something unique within ourselves. Show it, and wear it proudly. Let the one you like see the real you and find you interesting and attractive regardless. Get the help from the above tips and step up your game.

Chapter 17:

6 Habits of Ridiculously Likeable People

We all know someone with great influence on everyone he/she meets. They have the ability to change your mind in an instant. You cannot help but love them for who they are. Their charisma is unmatched and their enthusiasm is heavenly. To some, this is innate but to others, they build this character over time.

Here are 6 Habits of Ridiculously Likeable People:

1. They Are Talkative

Most likeable people are talkative. They never tire of talking about their experiences or their thoughts. It appears that they have nothing to hide and you can easily see through their lives. It is not easy to offend them because they say aloud their likes and dislikes even without anyone enquiring. Everyone around them would know what offends the talker in their midst and would keep off that lane.

Do you know that person at the office who would respectfully talk freely without any reservation? His/her colleagues cannot help but love them for who they are. Talkative people are like an open book and those they interact with are not afraid of them because their intentions are clear.

One misfortune that follows talkers is they are prone to attacks from unfriendly quarters. Their openness is a potential target for enemies. If you are a talkative person, beware of the information you give to others. Detailed personal information is not meant for everyone's ears.

Another disadvantage of talkers is that they may not be trusted with classified information because it is unsafe and unsecure with them. They may unintentionally give it away to the enemy.

Above all, talkative people are loveable to a fault. They speak boldly what others may not. They also lighten the gravity of matters if they are the ones to break such news.

2. They Are Friendly

Friendliness charms even the introverts. It is the right step towards developing healthy relationships. Who can afford to be offensive to a friendly person? Being friendly makes you likeable without any pre requisites. If you can hold a conversation with a stranger beyond greetings, then you are warmly receptive.

On the contrary, hostile people are not likeable because they are offensive and sometimes disrespectful. Hostility creates more enemies than friends – a bad environment for businesses and healthy relationships to thrive.

Friendly people easily create more friends wherever they go. They nature their relationships excellently and grow their network exponentially. They give no reason for anyone not to like them and sometimes turn their foes to allies.

3. They Are Happy Always

Happiness can neither be hidden nor faked. Happiness is also contagious. People will naturally want to be around those who add value to their lives. Your value is measured by the impact you have on those around you. Happy people are automatically loveable. How can you fail to love those who give you a dose of joy every day?

It is amazing the power that happy people wield over those they meet. Such influence does not come through coercion. The impact happy people have in the society, in boardrooms or in the pitch is significant. This makes them very pivotal in many matters and as a result, they win the hearts of many people.

The people who are mean and without humor achieve the contrary of what happy people do. They repel their audiences. Instead of winning the hearts of those they meet, they lose even the trust of those already in their fold.

Happy people are peace loving. Peace is the only avenue that happiness can thrive. A microscopic view of the DNA of ridiculously likeable people shows happiness engrained in the peace they enjoy. Everybody loves peace. By extension, that love will overflow to happy people.

4. They Are Charismatic

Charismatic people are charming to a fault. They are positively confident and not boastful in any manner. Such charisma makes them great influencers, drawing a large following. Renowned world leaders have this personality. Former US president, Barack Obama is a perfect example of a charismatic leader.

He is loved globally more even after he left office in 2016. His charity work does is not ignorable. Such charisma makes him ridiculously likeable. To be universally acceptable, cultivate the charismatic personality.

Like everything else, charisma too can be developed under the right conditions. With proportionate zeal, charisma can increase and consume any hate that may arise.

5. They Are Innocent

To be innocent is simply not to be guilty. Likeable people are free from any guilt of whatever form. Innocence is uncommon in the current world. When the world sees innocence, it is awed by it. People are attracted to what is not common. They will love those it sees innocent.

Who will associate with the guilty? None. If you manage to appeal to the public as innocent, you will be likeable by everyone. Innocent people are free from scandals. The perception that the public has on you is the determinant of innocence.

Scandalous individuals do not appeal to the public. How can you attract love from people when all you do is turn their rage towards you?

Innocence is not an act, but a habit. Do not engage in crime or social injustices. Always be at the forefront in condemning social ills. It will not make you any righteous, but it will prove that you champion the right ideals and make you stand out from the crowd that remains silent on injustices.

6. They Are Bold and Decisive

Boldness is making your stand known. It is not being timid. Bold people are loveable. They are loved because they speak out what others are afraid of saying. Their innocence to ills makes them bold to stand up for the weak and disadvantaged.

The public loves people who are uniquely able to handle what most of them cannot. Be clear in your decisions and do not sit on the fence. Ridiculously liked people attained the level of acceptance they enjoy from possibly a public decision they made on a matter of national or global interest. This set them apart and from then, they were marked for greatness.

Have you ever wondered what propelled great personalities to national or global acceptance? Well, the above are six habits of ridiculously liked people.

Chapter 18:

How to Love Yourself First

It's so easy to tell someone "Love yourself" and much more difficult to describe *how* to do it. Learn and practice these six steps to gradually start loving yourself more every day:

Step 1: Be willing to feel pain and take responsibility for your feelings.

Step 1 is mindfully following your breath to become present in your body and embrace all of your feelings. It's about moving toward your feelings rather than running away from them with various forms of self-abandonment, such as staying focused in your head, judging yourself, turning to addictions to numb out, etc. All feelings are informational.

Step 2: Move into the intent to learn.

Commit to learning about your emotions, even the ones that may be causing you pain, so that you can move into taking loving action.

Step 3: Learn about your false beliefs.

Step 3 is a deep and compassionate process of exploration—learning about your beliefs and behavior and what is happening with a person or situation that may be causing your pain. Ask your feeling self, your inner child: "What am I thinking or doing that's causing the painful feelings of anxiety, depression, guilt, shame, jealousy, anger, loneliness, or emptiness?" Allow the answer to come from inside, from your intuition and feelings.

Once you understand what you're thinking or doing that's causing these feelings, ask your ego about the fears and false beliefs leading to the self-abandoning thoughts and actions.

Step 4: Start a dialogue with your higher self.

It's not as hard to connect with your higher guidance as you may think. The key is to be open to learning about loving yourself. The answers may come immediately or over time. They may come in words or images or dreams. When your heart is open to learning, the answers will come.

Step 5: Take loving action.

Sometimes people think of "loving myself" as a feeling to be conjured up. A good way to look at loving yourself is by emphasizing the action: "What can I *do* to love myself?" rather than "How can I *feel* love for myself?"

By this point, you've already opened up to your pain, moved into learning, started a dialogue with your feelings, and tapped into your spiritual guidance. Step 5 involves taking one of the loving actions you identified in Step 4. However small they may seem at first, over time, these actions add up.

Step 6: Evaluate your action and begin again as needed.

Once you take the loving action, check in to see if your pain, anger, and shame are getting healed. If not, you go back through the steps until you discover the truth and loving actions that bring you peace, joy, and a deep sense of intrinsic worth.

Over time, you will discover that loving yourself improves everything in your life—your relationships, health and well-being, ability to manifest your dreams, and self-esteem. Loving and connecting with yourself is the key to loving and connecting with others and creating loving relationships. Loving yourself is the key to creating a passionate, fulfilled, and joyful life.

Chapter 19:

Confidence: The Art of Humble-Pride

There is a very fine line between confidence and overconfidence, being bold and being belligerent, having authority and having arrogance. It is a line that trips even the most nimble footed, but usually because they have dedicated no clear thoughts on how to manage it. Instead, they follow their gut on how far they can push or how much they should hold back. This is the paradox; you need to be confident. You need self-belief, you need to be assured of your ability and sometimes even certain of what the outcome will be. All of those things are empowering. In the words of Tony Robbins, you have to awaken the giant within. But had Goliath stooped to consider David's sling he would have worn a different helmet. The problem was that Goliath had a belief that he was fully capable of everything just as he was. I like to call it confidence without context, or universal, unanimous support of the self. That is the dangerous kind of confidence that spills over into arrogance. Chess grandmasters will tell you that the moment you assume you will win is the moment you lose. Because that is precisely when you start to make mistakes. You become too focussed on what your next move is that you don't even see theirs. You become so absorbed in your strategy that you fail to account for their plan and the bigger picture. It was confidence without context that made Goliath run straight towards to the flying stone.

Confidence without context is an assumption. And the problem with assumptions is that they go one step beyond the rationality of an expectation. Assumption goes into the fight drunk, having already celebrated the victory. But that leads to its inevitable demise. Expectation remains present, it acknowledges the reality of the situation. Assumption arrives intoxicated, expectation arrives in control. That is the difference. Pride is the greatest antidote to reason, which makes humility its greatest ally. If you want to stay in the fight you need to have both confidence and humility. If you want to stay competitive, if you want to get a promotion, if you want to level up. Whatever it is that you want, I can guarantee that the path to get there is a hopscotch of humility and confidence. Every bold step forward must be followed by a humble one. Note that humility does not take you backwards, it keeps you balanced. You can hop along in arrogance, but you will never last as long or be as strong as the one who keeps an even stride. If you strive for something, then you need to start striding towards it. And the rhythm of your march should beat to the sounds of a two-tone drum. Because confidence without context is like hopping up stairs – you might reach the second floor, but you will never manage the pyramid.

Chapter 20:

This Is Life

Who doesn't ponder the most basic and primary question, 'What is Life?' It is a bit cliche, but not unnecessary at all. And it certainly isn't illogical to think about what we are and what we have.

We often take life for granted but never realize what we have is special. We never contemplate the most important aspect of our existence.

We evolve during our time on this Earth. We start from nothing. But build towards a stronger being with greater and much better ambitions. We try to excel at everything we cross paths with. We strive towards our conscious development. We work towards our physical as well as emotional well-being.

We have a lot to live for but we rarely try to live for what matters the most. We never try to live like we have a greater purpose. Rather we try to go for petty things that might not even last for that long.

Life is short compared to what is going on around us. But we have to live it like there are unlimited seasons to come, each with its own blessings, each with its own opportunities.

We, humans, have evolved enough to be able to see beyond most plain things, but we chose to get soaked up in shallow waters. This life is a deep ocean with limits practically unpredictable.

Life is unexpected, it's unintentional, it's fussy but worth living for.

The life we see today is the collection of infinite, unbroken, and eternal events, rippling together simultaneously.

We say someone is alive when we see them breathing and moving but we never really know if that person is actually alive inside. We never really think about if the person is happy inside and enjoying what they have right now. We never try to look through the person and help them be alive for what matters.

Life never treats everyone the same way. But you don't need to get depressed every time you miss an alarm, or perform badly in an exam, or don't have the proper stats to show for your annual sales.

It doesn't always end badly and it certainly isn't bad every time of every day. It's just our psychology that makes us treat ourselves and life in a way that makes life demeaning and not worth it.

Everything is worth it once you try to look past the bad things and focus on the good ones you still get left with.

You have this one life, so go and live it like it matters the most to you. You might have to get a bit selfish and you might have to offend some people. Not deliberately, but just because you need some time and space which they might not allow, but it doesn't matter.

The epitome of life is that you have a clock ticking with each second getting you closer to the end. But you can still run around the clock and make it work as a swing. Enjoy with a purpose. Lead with your heart and you will come across wonders.

Chapter 21:

Happy People Find Reasons to Laugh and Forge Deep Connections

"...Making a connection with men and women through humour, happiness and laughter not only helps you make new friends, but it is the means to establish a strong, meaningful connection to people."

People always try to have a personality that attracts people and makes them feel comfortable around them. Utilizing their humour has been one of those ways to create new friendships. But once you start doing this, you will realize that this humorous nature has emotions and attitudes that comprise happiness and positivity. This will also help you create deep and meaningful connections that will last a lifetime.

When you intend to focus on humour to find deep connections, your subconscious mind starts focusing on positivity. You will slowly turn out to be more positive in your reasoning and conduct because awareness of what's funny is truly only demonstrative of one's very own bliss. In this manner, you're sustaining a more appealing, and that's just the beginning "contagious" attitude. Similarly, as we search out bliss in our everyday lives through satisfying work, leisure activities, individual interests and day to day life, so too do people seek out and wish to be encircled by joy on a relational level: joy and bitterness are contagious, and we as a whole wish to get the happy bug.

Humour helps fashion friendships since we wish to encircle ourselves with individuals who are glad. This way, our objective shouldn't just be to utilize humour to make new companions, however to zero in on the entirety of the uplifting perspectives and feelings that include an entertaining and carefree nature. By embodying satisfaction, inspiration, happiness, receptiveness and tranquillity, we sustain a more grounded and "contagious" state of being.

Historically there was a negative connotation attached to humour, but over the years, research was done, and it proved otherwise. In any case, research on humour has come into the daylight, with humour currently seen as a character strength. Good brain science, a field that analyzes what individuals progress admirably, notes that humour can be utilized to cause others to feel better, acquire closeness, or help buffer pressure. Alongside appreciation, expectation and otherworldliness, a funny bone has a place with the arrangement of qualities positive clinicians call greatness; together, they help us manufacture associations with the world and give significance to life. Enthusiasm for humour corresponds with different qualities, as well, like insight and love of learning. Furthermore, humour exercises or activities bring about expanded sensations of passionate prosperity and idealism.

Once you step into adulthood, it can be difficult for many people to form friendships and then keep up with them because all of us get busier in our lives. Still, it's never too much to go to a bar and strike up a conversation with a random person and believe us, if you have a good sense of humour, they will be naturally attracted towards you.

Chapter 22:
Deal With Your Fears Now

Fear is a strange thing.

Most of our fears are phantoms that never actually appear or become real,

Yet it holds such power over us that it stops us from making steps forward in our lives.

It is important to deal with fear as it not only holds you back but also keeps you caged in irrational limitations.

Your life is formed by what you think.

It is important not to dwell or worry about anything negative.

Don't sweat the small stuff, and it's all small stuff (Richard Carlson).

It's a good attitude to have when avoiding fear.

Fear can be used as a motivator for yourself.

If you're in your 30s, you will be in your 80s in 50 years, then it will be too late.

And that doesn't mean you will even have 50 years. Anything could happen.

But let's say you do, that's 50 years to make it and enjoy it.

But to enjoy it while you are still likely to be healthy, you have a maximum of 15 years to make it - minus sleep and living you are down to 3 years. If however you are in your 40s, you better get a move on quickly.

Does that fear not dwarf any possible fears you may have about taking action now?
Dealing with other fears becomes easy when the ticking clock is staring you in the face.
Most other fears are often irrational.

We are only born with two fears, the fear of falling and the fear of load noises.
The rest have been forced on us by environment or made up in our own minds.
The biggest percentage of fear never actually happens.

To overcome fear we must stare it in the face and walk through it knowing our success is at the other side.
Fear is a dream killer and often stops people from even trying.
Whenever you feel fear and think of quitting, imagine behind you is the ultimate fear of the clock ticking away your life.

If you stop you lose and the clock is a bigger monster than any fear.
If you let anything stop you the clock will catch you.

So stop letting these small phantoms prevent you from living,
They are stealing your seconds, minutes, hours , days and weeks.

If you carry on being scared, they will take your months, years and decades.

Before you know it they have stolen your life.

You are stronger than fear but you must display true strength that fear will be scared.

It will retreat from your path forever if you move in force towards it because fear is fear and by definition is scared.

We as humans are the scariest monsters on planet Earth.

So we should have nothing to fear

Fear tries to stop us from doing our life's work and that is unacceptable.

We must view life's fears as the imposters they are, mere illusions in our mind trying to control us.

We are in control here.

We have the free will to do it anyway despite fear.

Take control and fear will wither and disappear as if it was never here.

The control was always yours you just let fear steer you off your path.

Fear of failure, fear of success, fear of what people will think.

All irrational illusions.

All that matters is what you believe.

If your belief and faith in yourself is strong , fear will be no match for your will.

Les Brown describes fear as false evidence appearing real.

I've never seen a description so accurate.

Whenever fear rears its ugly head, just say to yourself this is false evidence appearing real.

Overcoming fear takes courage and strength in one's self.

We must develop more persistence than the resistance we will face when pursuing our dreams.

If we do not develop a thick skin and unwavering persistence we will be beaten by fear, loss and pain.

Our why must be so important that these imposters become small in comparison.

Because after all the life we want to live does dwarf any fears or set back that might be on the path.

Fear is insignificant.

Fear is just one thing of many we must beat into the ground to prove our worth.

Just another test that we must pass to gain our success.

Because success isn't your right,

You must fight

With all your grit and might

Make it through the night and shine your massive light on the world.

And show everyone you are a star.

Chapter 23:

8 Signs You Have Found Your Soulmate

"People think a soulmate is your perfect fit, and that's what everyone wants. But a true soulmate is a mirror, the person who shows you everything that is holding you back, the person who brings you to your attention so you can change your life." - Elizabeth Gilbert.

Legends say that even before you were born, the name of your spiritual half was determined. The two souls roam around the world to find their significant other. Whenever they find one another, they will unite, and their spirits would become one. But finding our long-lost soulmate isn't as easy as we think it is. Out of 7 billion people, it could take some time to find out our perfect match. However, when we meet them, we'll click with them instantly and just know in our hearts that they are made for us. A soulmate is someone you keep coming back to, no matter the struggles, challenges, obstacles, downfalls, or any of the circumstances. Everything would feel perfect with them. But how do you know if someone is your soulmate? You needn't worry! We have compiled for you below the signs that you may have found your soulmate.

1. They Would Bring The Best In You

Have your friends called you boring or a party pooper since you have entered adult life? Of course, you blame it all on the fact that you have grown up now and have responsibilities. But there's this one person who tends to bring out the fun and sassy side of yours. You feel so comfortable around them that you're even willing to try new things with them. They make your anxiety and fear go away in the blink of an eye. Be it singing songs loudly in the crowd, trying bungee jumping, or just packing up your bags and moving across the country with them to pursue your goals and dreams, they will strengthen you by supporting your decisions and being there for you.

2. They Won't Play Games With You

They won't be inconsistent with you, like making you feel special one day and ignoring you completely the next. You won't be questioning his feelings about you or putting yourself in a state of over-thinking. Sure, they won't make grand gestures like showing up at your window holding a guitar at 3 in the morning or putting up a billboard saying how much they love you (although we will happily accept both). Still, they will make you realize your worth in their life by always prioritizing you, making you happy, asking about you throughout the day, and paying close attention to whatever you say.

3. You Respect Each Other's Differences

When starting a new relationship, people tend to avoid or hold back specific thoughts, beliefs, or opinions. This is because, in the game of love, both of the couple's emotions are at stake. They don't speak their mind until and unless they're entirely comfortable with their partner. Your soulmate would always be open to change and respect your opinions and views, even if they disagree. They wouldn't ever implement their beliefs and ideas on you but would instead find comfort in knowing that you both don't have the same set of minds. It's essential to be on the same page with your partner on certain things, like the future, life goals, children, etc., but it's okay to have different moral and political views, as long as you both respect each other and it doesn't hurt the other's sentiments.

4. You Forgive Each Other

Being soulmates doesn't save you from the wrath of arguments and fights. Every relationship experiences indifference and frustration from time to time. But it is one of the things that makes your bond stronger with your partner. You both would rather sit and try to talk it through or sort it out instead of going to bed angry at each other. And when it comes to forgiving the other, you both would do it in a heartbeat. You wouldn't consider holding the other person guilty and would make unique gestures to try and make it up with them.

5. You Give Each Other Space

Your partner doesn't constantly bug you by texting and calling you every minute. They don't ask you about your whereabouts and don't act overly possessive. And rightly so, you do the same with them. You give each other your space and know that the other person would always be there for you. Even if you have to ask them about some distance, they respect it without complaining. You both trust each other with your whole heart and respect them enough to give them the space they have asked for.

6. You Empathize With Each Other

If your soulmate tells you about them getting good grades in college, finding their dream job, or getting a promotion, you find yourself being more excited and happier for them than they are. Sometimes, we feel drained out by showing too much empathy to other people and understanding and friendly. But with your soulmate, you don't have to force it out or pretend, and it just comes naturally. Whenever they feel scared or anxious, you're right there with them, protecting them from the world and not leaving their side until you make sure they're okay.

7. You Communicate With Each Other Effectively

They say that communication is essential for any long-lasting relationship. If you aren't communicating well with your partner, you might find yourself in the depths of overthinking the worst-case scenarios. Your partner makes it easy for you to share with them, even if you hadn't done the deed before. You find yourself talking about the tough things, the things that bother you or hurt you, and they comfort and console you reassure you that they will fix it. Similarly, you make sure your partner speaks your mind to you, and you do your best to right your wrongs and clear any of their doubts.

8. You Have Seen Each Other's Flaws And Still Loves Each Other The Same

It isn't easy to accept someone with the habits or traits that you despise. However, you have been your complete and utter authentic version of yourself with them, and they still love you the same. Be it crying loudly while watching an emotional sitcom, binge eating at night, snoring, burping, or just showing them your weak and vulnerable phase when you tend to push everyone away and dress up like a homeless drug addict. They find your quirks cute and accept you with all your imperfections and flaws, and you do the same with them.

Conclusion

A soulmate is someone who makes you realize your worth and brings out the best in you. They might drive you crazy, ignites your triggers, stirs your passions, but they might also be your most excellent teacher. They would allow you to discover your true self while always being there for you and supporting you all the way.

Chapter 24:

It's Not Your Job to Tell Yourself "No"

How many times have you had the chance to go around something that could have changed your life? What were your thoughts when you decided to enter a state where even the slightest thought of failure leads you to stop acting on it?

I'm sure every one of us has a good reason behind everything we opt to do or don't in our lives.

But there is never a good enough reason to back down just because we have some examples of failures on our hands.

No one can decide what reality and nature have decided for them. Everyone must learn to juggle life and play with every piece they get a hand on.

Everything in life is meant to be taken as a risk. You can never learn to swim till you get your first dive in a deep pool. You never learn to ride a bike till you have no one behind you to stop you from falling.

Everyone needs a bump every now and then. And when you finally decide to hike that hurdle, you finally start to see the horizon.

We all seem to get depressed more easily than we start to get motivated. We seem to get carried away with every stone that life throws back at us but we never try to catch that stone. We never try to indulge in one more suffering just to get better at what we are tested with.

Nobody wants to fail and that's why no one wants to take a chance at what might fail.

The mere fear of facing failure makes us build a mechanism of self-defense that forces us to say 'No' to anything that might hurt us one day.

But the reality is that it is illogical to stop just so you are afraid to face the reality. The reality is that you are a sane human and this is life. Life tests us in ways hardly imaginable.

When you say 'No' to yourself, it rarely means 'Not Now'. It always means 'Maybe some other time'. But deep down we already know that we will never attempt to do that thing. At least not consciously.

We always try for the best. We try to be the best at what we already have and are already doing. We are motivated enough to try new things, things that are more scary and unknown to us.

What we really should be doing is to try and get a taste of newer victories. Trying to search for new horizons. Trying to get what most fail to achieve. Because every other man or woman is just like us, afraid to fail and avoiding embarrassment. Our embarrassments are mostly self-imposed and we are the better judge of our failures.

There is no motivation and inspiration more powerful in the world than the spark that ignites within you.

Our sole purpose in life is to embrace everything that we come across. It is never to prevent something just because you don't have the courage to face your failures yet.

Chapter 25:

6 Ways To Get People To Like You

We are always trying for people to like us. We work on ourselves so that we can impress them. Everyone can not enjoy a single person. There will always be someone who dislikes them. But, that one person does not stop us from being charming and making people like us. In today's generation, good people are difficult to find. We all have our definition of being liked. We all have our type of person to select. That makes it very hard for someone to like someone by just knowing their name. We always judge people quickly, even to understand their nature. That makes it hard to like someone.

People always work their selves to be liked by the majority of people. It gives you a sense of comfort knowing that people are happy with you. You feel at ease when you know that people around you tend to smile by thinking about you. For that, you need to make an excellent first impression on people. Training yourself in such a way that you become everyone's favorite can sure be tiring. But, it always comes with a plus point.

1. Don't Judge

If you want people to like you, then you need to stop judging them. It is not good to consider someone based on rumors or by listening to one side of the story. Don't judge at all. We can never have an idea of what's going on in an individual life. We can not know what they are going through without them telling us. The best we can do is not judge them. Give them time to open up. Let them speak with you without the fear of being judged. Assuming someone is the worst without you them knowing is a horrendous thing to do.

2. Let Go of Your Ego and Arrogance

Make people feel like they can talk to you anytime they want. Arrogance will lead you nowhere. You will only be left alone in the end. So, make friends. Don't be picky about people. Try to get to know everyone with their own stories and theories. Make them feel comfortable around you to willingly come to talk to you and feel at ease after a few words with you. Being egotistic may make people fear you, but it will not make people like you. Be friendly with everyone around you.

3. Show Your Interest In People

When people talk about their lives, let them. Be interested in their lives, so it will make them feel unique around you. Make sure you listen attentively to their rant and remember as much as possible about a person. Even if they talk about something boring, try to make an effort towards them. If they talk about something worth knowledge, appreciate them. Ask them questions about it, or share your part of information with them, if you have any on that subject. Just try to make an effort, and people will like you instantly.

4. Try To Make New Friends

People admire others when they can click with anyone they meet. Making new friends can be a challenge, but it gives you confidence and, of course, new friends. Try to provide an excellent first impression and show them your best traits. Try to be yourself as much as possible, but do not go deep into friendship instantly. Give them time to adapt to your presence. You will notice that they will come to you themselves. That is because they like being around you. They trust you with their time, and you should valve it.

5. Be Positive

Everyone loves people. You give a bright, positive vibe. They tend to go to them, talk to them and listen to them. People who provide positive energy are easy to communicate with, and we can almost instantly become friends. Those are the type of people we can trust and enjoy being around. Positivity plays a critical role in your want to be liked. It may not be easy, but practice makes perfect. You have to give it your all and make everyone happy.

6. Be Physically and Mentally Present For The People Who Need You

People sometimes need support from their most trusted companion. You have to make sure you are there for them whenever they need you. Be there for them physically, and you can comfort someone without even speaking with them. Just hug them or just try to be there for them. It will make them feel peaceful by your presence. Or be there emotionally if they are ready. Try to talk to them. Listen to whatever they have to say, even if it doesn't make sense. And if they need comfort. Try to motivate them with your words.

Conclusion

You need to improve yourself immensely if you want people to like you. Make sure you do the right thing at the right time. Make people trust you and make them believe your words. Even a small gesture can make people like you. Have the courage to change yourself so that people will like you with all their heart's content.

Chapter 26:

Nothing Is Impossible

Success is a concept as individual as beauty is, in the eye of the beholder, but with each individuals success comes testing circumstances, the price that must be paid in advance.

The grind,

The pain and the losses all champions have endured.

These hardships are no reason to quit but an indicator that you are heading in the right direction, because we must walk through the rain to see the rainbow and we must endure loss to make space for our new desired results.

Often the bigger the desired change , the bigger the pain, and this is why so few do it.

The very fact that are listening to this right now says to me you have something extra about you.

Inside you know there is more for you and that dream you have, you believe it is possible.

If others have done it before, then so can you , because we can do anything we set our minds and hearts to.

But we must take control of our destiny, have clear results in mind and take calculated action towards those results.

The path may be foggy and unknown but as you commit to the result and believe in it the path, it will be revealed soon enough.

We don't need to know the how, to declare we are going to do something, the how will come later.

Clear commitment to the result is key .

Too many people never live their dreams because they don't know how.

The how can be found out always if we can commit and believe fully in the process.

Faith is the magic elixir to success, without it nothing is possible.

What you believe about you is everything

If you believe you cannot swim and your dream is to be an Olympic swimming champion, what are your chances?

Any rational person would say, well learn to swim,

How many of you want to be multi-millionaires?

I guess everyone?

How many out there know how to get to such a status?

Would we just give up and say it is impossible?

Or would it be as logical as simply learning how to swim or ride a bike?

We believe someone could be an Olympic swimming champion with training and practice , but not a multi-millionaire?

Many of us think big goals are simply too unrealistic.

Fear of failure , fear of what people might think , fear of change , all common reasons for aiming low in life.

But when we aim low and succeed the disappointment in that success is a foul tasting medicine.

Start gaining clarity in the reality of our results.

By thinking bigger we all have the ability to hit what seem now like unrealistic heights, but later realise that nothing is impossible.

We should all start from the assumption that we can do anything, it might take years of training but we can do it. Anything we set our minds to, we can do it.

So ask yourself right now those very important questions.

What exactly would I be doing right now that will make me the happiest person in the world? How much money do I want ?

What kind of relationships do I want?

When You have defined those things clearly,

Set the bar high and accept nothing less.

Because life will pay you any price.

But the time is ticking, you can't have it twice.

Chapter 27:

10 Facts About Attraction

Everything from taking an interest in someone to admire someone physically or mentally is known as an attraction. The attraction could be a romantic or sexual feeling. Attraction can be confusing and takes time to understand. Most of us find it hard to know what we feel about or are attracted to someone. We couldn't figure out what type of attraction it is, but we should remember there is no right way to feel the attraction. There are so many types of attraction, and some could happen at once.

1. Women Attracted To Older Men

So, it is expected that most women these days are attracted to older men just because of their "daddy issues" and the most one is the financial issue but according to study it's not the reason. According to authentic references or studies, the women born to old fathers are attracted to older men, and the women born to younger men are attracted to younger men. As they think that they will treat them just like their father did.

2. Opposite Attraction

As we all heard before, "opposite attracts." well, it is true, according to a study of the university of dresden, that both men and women are attracted to different leukocyte antigens, which is also known as the hla complex. A genetic blueprint responsible for the immune function is so unique that this attraction has to do with species' survival. Now, how do our brains detect the opposite hla complex?

According to a study, our brain can see the opposite hla complex only by the scents; isn't it a fascinating fact?

3. The Tone Of Women's Voices

According to a study by the university of canada, when women flirt, their voice pitch increases automatically. Not only while flirting, but women's voice tones increase at different emotions. The highest tone of a woman's voice gets when she is fertile or ovulated, and guess what? According to studies, men like the most high-pitched voices of women.

4. Whisper In The Left Ear

According to a study, when you want to intimate someone, like whispering " i love you" in their ear, then whisper in their left ear because whispering in the left ear has 6% more effect than a whisper in the right one.

5. Red Dress

Red dress attracts both men and women. It is examined in a study that usually men love women in the red dress. They find it intimidating.

6. Men With Beard

Women find men attractive with a beard. Beard with the subtle cut. Another fantastic fact about the beard is that women judged men with a beard to be a better choice for a long-term relationship. This might be because men with beards look more mature and responsible. Beard also makes you look like you have a higher status in society.

7. Men Trying To Sound Sexy

So, women have no trouble whatsoever changing their voice, but men have no clue about it. Women lower their voice pitch and make it sexy, and men find it so attractive, but men find it very difficult to sound sexy. It got a little bit worse when men tried to say sexy. The reason behind this is elaborated in research, according to which men are not focused on making their voice sexy but women do.

8. Competing

Research shows that when you are famous for everyone, and everyone likes them, you get attracted to them and try to get them. You start competing for that person with other people, which makes you feel more attracted to that person. That person will be in your head all the time because you see everyone admiring and chasing that person.

9. Adrenaline:

Studies show that adrenaline has to do a lot with attraction. People find others more attractive when they are on an adrenaline rush themselves. According to a study, women find men more attractive when they are ovulating than in another period.

10. Weights And Heights

When taking a liking to someone. People always prefer to choose a person who holds the right weight and height according to them. Different people may have different opinions. When they find a person with a likable body, they get easily attracted to them.

Conclusion

Attraction to someone can play a significant role in getting them. When people are attracted to you, they make you feel worth it all, and you feel ecstatic. Attraction can be=ring in a lot of factors like popularity, relationship and of course, love.

Chapter 28:
Make Time for Your Partner

When I first got into my relationship, I thought my boyfriend and my 100-hour workweek would have to battle it out until the bitter end. Yet somehow, I've managed to maintain both. It turns out there are a lot of weird ways to make time for your partner when you're busy AF. You may have to get creative and resort to some weird measures, but I am living proof that there is no such thing as being too busy for your loved ones.

We all have to run errands. That time is gone from your workday anyway. So, why not use it to show your partner you care instead of just getting what you need? Picking up each other's shampoo and favorite cereal (or, perhaps more practically, take turns picking up groceries and toiletries for the both of you) is one way to connect without needing to make any more time in your schedule.

You spend the same amount of time cooking for two people as you do for one, but since you're feeding two, you *save* time by doing this. Think about it: Instead of cooking every night, you only have to do it every *other* night. Even if you both eat it in front of your computers, making food for each other is a loving gesture that'll make you appreciate each other.

If you live together, you'll probably be sleeping in the same bed anyway. But even if you don't, your dates can consist solely of sleeping if that's what it takes to make time for each other. Or, if you can't sleep through the night with someone else next to you, you can try just sharing nap time.

Even if you don't get around to working out that much, the time you can devote to exercise will help clear your mind, so it's worthwhile if you can make it out for a short run or yoga class. Plus, working out together can boost your attraction by releasing endorphins.

I can't always handle this, especially when I need to feel like nobody wants my attention to focus. But for less intensive tasks, it can be comforting to cuddle up to your significant other while you're working. You can even be each other's sounding boards if you need help coming up with ideas.

This one will not work for everyone. But if you have an office in a similar place, your walk or ride to work can be your bonding time, even if it's just part of the way. Even just a shared walk to the train station can pay off if you think ahead enough to coordinate your trips to and from work.

Chapter 29:
7 Ways On How To Attract Success In Life

Successful people fail more times than unsuccessful people try. A new thought author and metaphysical writer Florence Scovel Shinn in her timeless 1940 novel, 'the secret door to success,' suggests that "Success is not a secret, it is a system." Throughout the centuries, the leaders have alluded to the possibility that success can be attracted into one's life simply by thinking and doing. It is rather a planned journey as we give validity to the premise of creating a plan or setting a goal for ourselves. Goals are set to be achieved, and achievements pave the way for success. Here are 7 Ways To Attract Success In Your Life:

1. Define What Success Means To You

Success is subjective to the person who seeks to obtain it, and the ideas may be different for each other. For some of us, success means wealth. For some, it means health and happiness. While for some, it is the mere effort of getting out of bed every day. But the thing that is most highlighted is that we can never get success without struggling. Every one of us wants success, but we do not know how to bring about that life-changing phenomenon that will take us to the zenith of our potential.

2. Begin With Gratitude

From flying to the sky to crashing to the ground, be always thankful to wherever life takes you. Always start by being grateful for what you already have. Whether it's good or bad, we cannot climb the stairs of success without having experiences. If we make mistakes, we should make sure not to give up, rather learn from those mistakes. We must strive to embrace our flaws and imperfections. If we tend to fall seven times, we must have the energy to get up eight times. Whatever life throws us at, no matter the obstacles and challenges, we should always be in a state of gratitude and always be thankful for our learning.

3. Stop Making Excuses

Your decisions lead to your destiny. If you are thinking about delaying your work or 'chilling' first, then someone else will take that opportunity for himself. You either grab on the opportunities from both hands, or you sit on the sidelines and watch someone else steal your spotlight. There's no concept of resting and being lazy when you have to work towards your goals and achieve your dreams. One of the major mistakes of unsuccessful people is that they make endless excuses. They would avoid their tasks in any way instead of working on them and actually doing them. You will attract success only if you put your mind towards something and work hard towards it.

4. Realize Your Potential

The fine line between incredibly hardworking people and yet fail to achieve success, and the ones who are at the peak of their respective field is simple – potential. We never realize our true potential until we are put in a situation where there's no way out but to express our abilities. We might think that people have more excellent skills than us or have more knowledge than us. But the truth is, we have more potential inside of us. This might be tougher to implement as we don't know how well we can handle things while stressing out or how much hidden talents and skills we possess. Our potential is merely what might make us successful or a failure. It all depends on how much we are willing to try and push ourselves forward.

5. Celebrate The Success Of Others

What you wish upon others finds its way and comes back to you again. While seeing people being successful in their professional and personal lives and making a fortune in their careers and businesses can be tough on our lives, always remember that they too faced struggles and challenges before reaching here. There's no need to be envious as life has an abundance of everything to offer to everyone. Whatever is it in your destiny will always find its way to you. You can't snatch what others have achieved, and similarly, others can't seize whatever that you have or may achieve. Congratulate people around you and be excited for them. Send out positive vibes to everyone so you may receive the same.

6. Behave As If You Are Successful

Have you heard of the term "fake it till you make it?" Well, it applies to this scenario too. You can fake your success and act like a successful person until you really become one. First, surround yourself with lucrative people. See what habits they have developed over time, how they dress up, how they behave, and, most importantly, how much work they do daily to achieve their goals. Get inspired from them and adopt their healthy habits. Be successful in your own eyes first so that eventually you can be successful in other's eyes as well.

7. Provide Value For Others

While money and fame are the most common success goals, we should first try to focus on creating value in the world. A lot of successful people wanted to change things in the world first and help people out. Mark Zuckerberg built a tool for Harvard students initially and now has over 1.4 billion users. The first thing on our mind after waking up shouldn't be money or success, and it would be to create value for the world and the people around us.

Conclusion

It would be best if you strived to explore the unique, endless possibilities within you. Then, when you start working on yourself, you're adding to your mind's youth, vitality, and beauty.

Chapter 30:
7 Ways To Keep Your Relationship Fresh And Exciting

At the beginning of a relationship, one can feel the excitement and the sparks that come from the newness of a relationship. For example, the butterflies you feel before going on a date can make you feel surprisingly on top of the world. It is the start of a relationship that makes you feel this way. At the beginning of a relationship, everything feels fresh as your partner surprises you and makes you feel special.

But as time goes on, the relationship becomes boring. This can often lead to an end of a relationship; to prevent this, you could always keep your relationship fresh and exciting. Even though now both of you are not the same person you used to be in each other's eyes, but you could still maintain that tingly sensation by trying to be more surprising.

Here are seven ways to keep your relationship fresh and exciting.

1. Keep Surprising Each Other

At the start of every relationship, partners often surprise each other with flowers, gifts, or a surprise date. These surprises cause the other partner to feel beloved. Still, people usually stop surprising their partners with such things as time goes on. By continuing to surprise your partner with gifts, flowers, and sweet notes, you keep your relationship fresh. After a while, you learn about the likes and dislikes of your partner. You can easily use that to your advantage by buying them flowers they like or small presents that make them happy. The happiness caused by these small gestures of love can keep the relationship from becoming dull. So don't let the element of surprise die.

2. Ask Them Out On A Date

A relationship often begins with a date, and the date makes you feel nervous and excited. Meeting your partner for the first few times can make you want to look the best version of yourself and continue your efforts to look and be the best for your partners. So don't stop the efforts. Ask your partner out on a fancy date to make them happy. Even if you are just ordering food from outside, you could still light up some candles and set the table with a fancy dinner set. This could make your partner feel special, and the freshness of the relationship doesn't die with time.

3. Try Something New Together

Always try to do something new, like watching movies you liked as a teenager or eating something you haven't tried before; it awakes the excitement your partner feels throughout the day. Try going ice skating or skateboarding together as a fun activity, taking time from your adult routine, and going hiking and other activities to have fun together simply.

4. Speak About Your Feelings Towards Them

Try voicing your thoughts about them. Don't shy away from words and tell them or remind them regularly how much they mean to you or how strongly you feel towards them; simple sentences like "I love you" can profoundly affect your partner. Please don't take your partner for granted but make them feel good about themselves and tell them how important they are in your life. This can make them appreciate your presence, and the relationship will remain fresh.

5. Set Life Goals Together

You and your partner can decide on some goals that you can achieve together as a couple. It can be any goal, as a financial goal, or exploring the world together. You could save money for vacations together. During this journey, you can motivate each other but can still have fun. Moreover, when you work as a team, it will also strengthen your bond.

6. Turn Off Your Phone

When spending time with each other, try turning off your phone. This will show your partner how important they are to you. Focus on their words and respond actively. Studies show that a relationship can end when you are more focused on social media apps than on your partner. Using too many social media apps can distance you from your partner; try spending more time with them than using your mobile phone and reestablish your bond with them.

7. Greet Each Other With Excitement

When a relationship begins, we often see couples embracing each other with love and passion even when they met just yesterday. Still, as time passes, couples can be seen greeting each other with just a simple hello or a short hug. Greeting your partner with excitement and enthusiasm can make them long to meet you. They would be excited all day long because of the way you greet them. This can ensure that the excitement of the relationship doesn't die. You can greet them with a warm, comforting hug or simply a few exciting words; saying mushy things can also make them feel loved, like "I missed you" when they come back home from work.

By following the above ways, you can keep your partner happy and your relationship fresh and exciting.

Chapter 31:

7 Ways To Deal With Sexual Problems In a Relationship

Whether the problem is big or small, there are as many things as you can do to get your sex life back on track. Your sexual well-being goes hand in hand with your overall emotional, physical, and mental health. Sexual dysfunction is defined as the difficulty or issue that might arise for an individual as well as for the couple during any stage of intimacy. It is an overly stigmatized situation that is far more common than many people realize. Overcoming sexual dysfunction doesn't have to be as daunting as it may feel. There are many ways to handle the frustration without putting too much strain on your partner or the relationship.

Communicating with your partner, availing yourself of some of the many excellent self-help materials on the market, maintaining a healthy lifestyle, and just having it easy and fun can help you weather tough times. Here are some ways to deal with the sexual problems in your relationship.

1. Know The Importance of Intimacy

It is essential to notice when the intimacy starts to wane within their relationship. Couples need to understand that they won't have the same level of sexual drive or desires throughout their relationship. Intimacy is a significant element to help couples bond. We feel calm and connected when we experience love and physical contact. If you have started to feel like you and your partner are experiencing intimacy issues, address them and don't hide them out of sheer embarrassment and shame.

2. Remember That You Are Not Alone

Sexual dysfunction in all its forms is something that plagues countless couples. There's no need to feel isolated. There are always ups and downs in every couple's sex life, and the real problem arises when they don't know how to talk about sex or the issues related to it. The societal stigma surrounding sexual dysfunction and lack of communication skills and education serve as the basis for why the couples feel ashamed and isolated in addressing their issues.

3. Get Educated

Couples mainly set up unrealistic expectations about sex that lead them to nothing but disappointment. Couples need to realize that their sexual desires, preferences, and abilities will begin to change as they age. A couple should get themselves informed about sexuality, sexual intercourse, and sexual dysfunction to be well aware of the challenges that they are facing or might face ahead. An excellent way to get educated is by contacting a sex therapist or reading books if you are too shy to talk openly about it.

4. Don't Play The Blame Game

Suppose the challenges you're facing affect one partner only. In that case, it is significant to face the issue as a team and work through it together. It is critical to look at sexual dysfunction as a couple experiencing a problem, and not just one partner. There is nothing worse than blaming and isolating your partner. Without the said support and communication, the problem is more likely to be increased than to dissolve.

5. Communicate With Care

Don't attempt to discuss your sexual problems with your partner if they are already stressed out about something else. Remember, timing is everything. Carefully address the problem with your partner and choose soft words to convey your message. Before engaging in the discussion, make sure both of you are level-headed, calm, well-rested, and prepared to have the conversation. It could get quite emotional, so you both have to be careful.

6. Give Yourself Time

As you age, your sexual responses slow down, and it may need more time for you to get aroused. The physical changes in your body might now give a completely different perspective of your sexual desires and arousals. Working on these physical necessities into your lovemaking routine can open doors to a new kind of sexual experience for you.

7. Do Kegel Exercises

Improving sexual fitness is essential for both men and women. They can do so by exercising their pelvic floor muscles. To engage in these exercises, tighten the muscle you would use to stop the urine in midstream. Hold the contraction for 2-3 seconds and then release. Repeat this ten times, doing a set of five each day. These exercises can be done anywhere, whether driving, standing in a checking line, or sitting at home.

Conclusion

Sexual dysfunction might be one of the hardest things to overcome in a relationship and is undoubtedly one of the most challenging issues to communicate with your partner about. However, with a bit of hard work, and a lot of support and love from your significant other, there is always a hope that you and your partner will find a solution that will eventually bring back happiness into your lives.

CPSIA information can be obtained
at www.ICGtesting.com
Printed in the USA
LVHW080933020822
724960LV00009B/485